by Iain Gray

Lang**Syne**

PUBLISHING

· WRITING *to* REMEMBER

WRITING *to* REMEMBER

79 Main Street, Newtongrange,
Midlothian EH22 4NA
Tel: 0131 344 0414   Fax: 0845 075 6085
E-mail: info@lang-syne.co.uk
www.langsyneshop.co.uk

Design by Dorothy Meikle
Printed by Ricoh Print Scotland
© Lang Syne Publishers Ltd 2012

ISBN 978-1-85217-203-9

Black

Echoes of a far distant past
can still be found in most names

Chapter one:

Origins of Scottish surnames

by George Forbes

It all began with the Normans.

For it was they who introduced surnames into common usage more than a thousand years ago, initially based on the title of their estates, local villages and chateaux in France to distinguish and identify these landholdings, usually acquired at the point of a bloodstained sword.

Such grand descriptions also helped enhance the prestige of these arrogant warlords and generally glorify their lofty positions high above the humble serfs slaving away below in the pecking order who only had single names, often with Biblical connotations as in Pierre and Jacques.

The only descriptive distinctions among this peasantry concerned their occupations, like Pierre the swineherd or Jacques the ferryman.

The Normans themselves were originally Vikings (or Northmen) who raided, colonised and eventually settled down around the French coastline.

They had sailed up the Seine in their longboats in 900AD under their ferocious leader Rollo and ruled the roost in north east France before sailing over to conquer England, bringing their relatively new tradition of having surnames with them.

It took another hundred years for the Normans to percolate northwards and surnames did not begin to appear in Scotland until the thirteenth century.

These adventurous knights brought an aura of chivalry with them and it was said no damsel of any distinction would marry a man unless he had at least two names.

The family names included that of Scotland's great hero Robert De Brus and his compatriots were warriors from families like the De Morevils, De Umphravils, De Berkelais, De Quincis, De Viponts and De Vaux.

As the knights settled the boundaries of

their vast estates, they took territorial names, as in Hamilton, Moray, Crawford, Cunningham, Dunbar, Ross, Wemyss, Dundas, Galloway, Renfrew, Greenhill, Hazelwood, Sandylands and Church-hill.

Other names, though not with any obvious geographical or topographical features, nevertheless derived from ancient parishes like Douglas, Forbes, Dalyell and Guthrie.

Other surnames were coined in connection with occupations, castles or legendary deeds. Stuart originated in the word steward, a prestigious post which was an integral part of any large medieval household. The same applied to Cooks, Chamberlains, Constables and Porters.

Borders towns and forts – needed in areas like the Debateable Lands which were constantly fought over by feuding local families – had their own distinctive names; and it was often from them that the resident groups took their communal titles, as in the Grahams of Annandale, the Elliots and Armstrongs of the East Marches, the Scotts and Kerrs of Teviotdale and Eskdale.

Even physical attributes crept into surnames, as in Small, Little and More (the latter being 'beg' in Gaelic), Long or Lang, Stark, Stout, Strong or Strang and even Jolly.

Mieklejohns would have had the strength of several men, while Littlejohn was named after the legendary sidekick of Robin Hood.

Colours got into the act with Black, White, Grey, Brown and Green (Red developed into Reid, Ruddy or Ruddiman). Blue was rare and nobody ever wanted to be associated with yellow.

Pompous worthies took the name Wiseman, Goodman and Goodall.

Words intimating the sons of leading figures were soon affiliated into the language as in Johnson, Adamson, Richardson and Thomson, while the Norman equivalent of Fitz (from the French-Latin 'filius' meaning 'son') cropped up in Fitzmaurice and Fitzgerald.

The prefix 'Mac' was 'son of' in Gaelic and clans often originated with occupations – as in MacNab being sons of the Abbot, MacPherson and MacVicar being sons of the minister and MacIntosh being sons of the chief.

The church's influence could be found in the names Kirk, Clerk, Clarke, Bishop, Friar and Monk. Proctor came from a church official, Singer and Sangster from choristers, Gilchrist and Gillies from Christ's servant, Mitchell, Gilmory and Gilmour from servants of St Michael and Mary, Malcolm from a servant of Columba and Gillespie from a bishop's servant.

The rudimentary medical profession was represented by Barber (a trade which also once included dentistry and surgery) as well as Leech or Leitch.

Businessmen produced Merchants, Mercers, Monypennies, Chapmans, Sellers and Scales, while down at the old village watermill the names that cropped up included Miller, Walker and Fuller.

Other self explanatory trades included Coopers, Brands, Barkers, Tanners, Skinners, Brewsters and Brewers, Tailors, Saddlers, Wrights, Cartwrights, Smiths, Harpers, Joiners, Sawyers, Masons and Plumbers.

Even the scenery was utilised as in Craig, Moor, Hill, Glen, Wood and Forrest.

Rank, whether high or low, took its place with Laird, Barron, Knight, Tennant, Farmer, Husband, Granger, Grieve, Shepherd, Shearer and Fletcher.

The hunt and the chase supplied Hunter, Falconer, Fowler, Fox, Forrester, Archer and Spearman.

The renowned medieval historian Froissart, who eulogised about the romantic deeds of chivalry (and who condemned Scotland as being a poverty stricken wasteland), once sniffily dismissed the peasantry of his native France as the jacquerie (or the jacques-without-names) but it was these same humble folk who ended up over-throwing the arrogant aristocracy.

In the olden days, only the blueblooded knights of antiquity were entitled to full, proper names, both Christian and surnames, but with the passing of time and a more egalitarian, less feudal atmosphere, more respectful and worthy titles spread throughout the populace as a whole.

Echoes of a far distant past can still be found in most names and they can be borne with pride in commemoration of past generations who fought and toiled in some capacity or other to make our nation what it now is, for good or ill.

Chapter two:

By fire and sword

Originally a common name to denote a person's complexion or hair colouring, there is nothing ordinary, however, about the lives and times of those who have borne the surname Black in all its varieties of spelling down through the centuries.

This is particularly so in Scotland, where Blacks not only established themselves in the rich and fertile Lowlands, but in the mists and mountains of the Highlands and Islands.

This Highland heritage arises through their links with no less than three famed clans, the proud MacGregors, Lamonts, and Macleans.

'Black' itself stems from the Old English word 'bleac', and variations include Blak, Blackie, Blaik, Blaikie, and Blake. Complicating matters, however, is that 'Blake' stems from an Old Norse word, 'bleikr', meaning white, or pale – the direct opposite of Black!

With a somewhat anarchic system of spelling in earlier centuries, it is now practically impossible to distinguish the original 'Blacks' from the original 'Blakes.'

Early Latin charters help to clarify matters, as the Latinised version of 'Black' is 'Niger', and this form of the surname is found in Scottish records from the early thirteenth to the late fifteenth centuries.

A Hugh Niger is recorded as having witnessed a charter in Fife in the first decade of the thirteenth century, while further south a James Blak and a William Blake are recorded in the bustling market town of Lanark in 1498.

The Gaelic form of black is 'dhuibh', and from this stems Mac Gille dhuibh ('son of the black lad'). This gives rise to the surnames of Macilduy, Macildowie, and MacGilledow. Other Gaelic renderings are Douie and Huie.

In the great dispersal from the Highlands to the Lowlands and even further afield that occurred from the mid-eighteenth century onwards, many of these Macilduys,

Macildowies, MacGilledows, Douies and Huies later adopted the anglicised form of Black.

The Blacks are recognised as a sept, or branch, of the three Highland clans of MacGregor, Lamont, and Maclean, and the reasons why the name came to be linked with these clans, particularly in the case of the MacGregors and the Lamonts, are rooted in tragedy and remain a stain on Scotland's historical record.

'S'rioghal mo dhream' (Royal is my blood) is the proud and defiant motto, while a lion's head bearing a five-point crown is the crest of the MacGregors, whose dim and distant roots are in Argyll and the secluded valleys of western Perthshire.

The MacGregor influence waned as more powerful clans encroached on their domains, until they became mere tenants on what had been from time immemorial their ancestral homelands.

This subservient role did not sit well with this clan of royal blood, and their passions and frustrations found an outlet in raiding and pillaging their neighbours.

Their widespread depredations reached such a level that in both 1562 and 1564, during the reign of Mary, Queen of Scots, chiefs of the affected clans were officially sanctioned to punish the MacGregors 'by fire and sword.'

This proved to have little effect, however, but more than twenty years later, in 1587, Mary's son, James VI, frustrated by the lawless state of affairs in the western Highlands, issued orders 'to pursue and prosecute with all vigour and extremity the wicked and unhappy race of Clan Gregor.'

Matters came to a head in February of 1603 when, horrified by a raid on the Colquhouns at Glenfruin, near Dumbarton, in which the MacGregors slaughtered 200 of the clan and made off with a rich booty of cattle, horses, goats, and sheep, a special Act of Council was passed that proscribed and prohibited the very name of MacGregor.

The chief, MacGregor of Glenstrae, was hanged along with eleven of his leading kinsmen and prices were put on the heads of other clans-

men, who could gain a pardon if they brought in
the head of a fellow clansman.

Eight years later, in 1611, a commission
was given to the Duke of Argyll to 'root out and
extirpate' all MacGregors and any who collabo-
rated with them.

Attempts were made to forcibly remove
MacGregor women and children to the
Lowlands, while MacGregor wives were brand-
ed on the face with a red-hot key.

No more than four MacGregors were
allowed to band together at any one time, while
the only 'weapon' they were allowed to carry was
a knife without a point to allow them to cut their
meat.

These harsh laws against the clan were re-enacted again in 1617, 1635, 1693, and after the abortive Jacobite Rising of 1745, when two companies of the clan from Balquhidder fought with distinction for the doomed cause of Prince Charles Edward Stuart.

The proscriptions against the clan were not lifted until 1774 and, in the interim, many MacGregors had been forced to adopt new names – most commonly 'neutral' surnames such as White, Brown, and Black.

In Gaelic, of course, the chosen form of 'Black' would have been Macilduy, Macildowie, MacGilledow, Douie, and Huie. These were later anglicised to Black.

Any Blacks of today who can trace a descent back to any of these Gaelic renderings of Black, or a descent back to Argyll or the valleys of western Perthshire, may well be descendants of those proud MacGregors who were faced with no option but conceal their true identities under the cover of a new name.

Chapter three:

Massacre and atrocity

The association of the surname Black to the Lamonts is as tragic as that of its connection to the MacGregors.

'Neither spare nor disgrace' is the motto, and an upright hand with the palm facing outwards is the crest of this clan that first appeared in the early thirteenth century in the Cowal region of Argyll, on Scotland's west coast.

Boasting an ancient Celtic pedigree that can be traced back to a branch of the famed royal house of the O'Neils of Ulster, the Lamonts progressively began to suffer from the encroachments of their more powerful Campbell neighbours.

In 1643, during the bloody strife between Crown and Covenant, Charles I issued a commission to his loyal supporter Sir James Lamont of Inveryne, Chief of Clan Lamont, to levy his forces against the monarch's enemies, in particular the Marquis of Argyll.

Argyll was the head of Clan Campbell and leader of those Covenanters who took their name from the National Covenant of 1638, which pledged to uphold the Presbyterian religion.

Sir James set about his task with zeal, slaughtering, for example, practically all of the inhabitants of the Campbell town of Strachur.

Following the defeat of the Royalist forces led by James Graham, Marquis of Montrose, at Philiphaugh, near Selkirk, in September of 1645, Sir James disbanded his forces and returned to his stronghold of Toward Castle, south of Inellan.

The Marquis of Argyll, meanwhile, quickly made himself master of Scotland and sought vengeance on his Lamont neighbours by besieging Toward Castle.

Sir James had no option but to agree to surrender, on June 3, 1646, but only after receiving a solemn assurance that his kinsfolk would be protected and his estates spared from plunder and destruction.

But Argyll reneged on the deal, and Sir

The First Marquis of Montrose

James Graham, the fifth Earl and first
Marquis of Montrose

James and his closest relatives were thrown into confinement. A more terrible fate awaited his kinsfolk, when 200 of them (some sources say 250) were herded up, cast into boats, and taken north to Dunoon.

Arriving at a hill known as Tom-a-Mhoir which, ironically, is the Gaelic for 'Hill of Justice', nearly 40 men described as 'leading gentlemen' of the Lamonts were summarily hanged from an ash tree that grew behind a near-by churchyard.

They were cut down while still alive and thrown into hastily dug pits, while the remainder of the captives, including women and children, were stabbed and bludgeoned and also thrown into the pits.

They were left to slowly suffocate to death after earth was thrown over them. A memorial to this massacre was erected on the southern outskirts of Dunoon in 1906 by the Clan Lamont Society (Scotland).

The Lamont lands on Cowal were then ravaged by the Campbells, with a number of clanswomen who had escaped the deportation to Dunoon hunted down and killed and their mutilated bodies left 'for prey to ravenous beasts and fowls.'

Sir James Lamont was forced to sign a humiliating document surrendering all his estates, and was not released from captivity until 1651, when the forces of Oliver Cromwell occupied Scotland.

Hunted down like wild beasts following the massacre at Dunoon, surviving Lamonts were driven from their lands and, in a desperate act of self-preservation, were forced to assume new identities, in common with the MacGregors, by taking on new surnames such as Black, White, or Brown.

Any Blacks of today who can trace a descent back to Cowal, in Argyll, could well be descendants of these original Lamonts.

It was also the fate of Blacks associated with Clan Maclean to become victims of an atrocity in 1586. A fortified tower is the crest, and 'Virtue mine honour' the motto of Clan Maclean, who claim descent from the monarchs of the ancient kingdom of Dalriada.

Supporters of the cause of Scotland's freedom during the Wars of Independence with England, Macleans fought at the side of the great warrior king Robert the Bruce at Bannockburn, and for centuries their main stronghold was on the west coast island of Mull.

The island of Gometra lies off Mull and was home to Macilduys/Douies/Huies, (later anglicised to 'Black'), many of whom later moved to the island of Lismore, and Clan Maclean recognises only these 'Blacks' as a sept of the clan.

A feud developed between the Macleans and their neighbouring MacDonalds, particularly after the MacDonald Lordship of the Isles was annexed to the Crown under James IV in 1493, and a struggle developed to fill the resultant power vacuum.

This set the Macleans and the MacDonalds at odds over the right to ownership of various lands.

The feud reached a murderous climax in the summer of 1586 after Angus MacDonald of Islay had accepted an invitation to share in the hospitality of Lachlan Maclean at his stronghold of Duart Castle, on Mull.

The traditional rules of hospitality were abruptly overturned after Maclean, whose sister was married to MacDonald, imprisoned his brother-in-law and his men.

They were released only after MacDonald agreed to renounce his claims to certain lands, including lands on Islay.

This was an act for which MacDonald would reap a grim vengeance when, some time later, Maclean, along with a 45-strong retinue that would have included his kinsmen from Gometra, travelled to take possession of the lands he had acquired on Mull.

Maclean had already taken MacDonald's young son as a hostage for his safety, but this proved to be worthless. He accepted hospitality at MacDonald's house of Mullintrea, he and his kinsfolk being lavishly wined and dined until they retired for the night to a long wooden hut that had been allocated for their accommodation.

They were awoken from their drunken slumbers, however, when MacDonald and about 200 of his clansmen surrounded the hut and ordered them to come out.

Maclean was taken prisoner and saved from immediate death only through the intervention of his nephew, but two of his kinsfolk who refused to leave the hut were roasted alive as it was burned down about their ears.

The remaining 43 of Maclean's clansmen and kinsfolk, including those from Gometra who would later be known under the anglicised surname of Black, were beheaded, some sources say at the rate of one a day, with the distraught Maclean forced to watch.

On the day allotted for his own barbaric execution, he was saved only after his tormentor broke a leg after falling from his horse, allowing time for the intervention of the acting head of Clan Campbell and a king's messenger to save his life.

His brother-in-law released Maclean, but only after he received an assurance he would be pardoned for his heinous crimes. Maclean, perhaps understandably, was no sooner free than he raised others of his kinsfolk and ravaged Islay by fire and sword.

MacDonald, predictably, exacted vengeance by ravaging both Mull and Tiree 'killing every human inhabitant and every wild beast that fell into his hands.'

Although the Blacks shared for centuries in the fortunes and misfortunes of the MacGregors, Lamonts, and Macleans and are recognised as septs of all three (with, as we have seen, some qualification in the case of the Macleans) Blacks of today are recommended by experts in such matters to adopt the Lamont tartan.

Chapter four:

Kindred of Black

Blacks have, in more peaceful times, made a significant contribution on an international scale in a variety of fields.

Researchers into the origins and history of surnames owe a huge debt to the efforts of George Fraser Black, who published his monumental *The Surnames of Scotland* in 1946, after 40 years of exhaustive research.

Born in Stirlingshire in 1866, Black immigrated to America, where he worked for thirty-five years with the New York Public Library. He died in 1948.

In the world of science, Joseph Black (1728-1799), who was born in Bordeaux, France, of Scottish parents but who later taught at both Glasgow and Edinburgh universities, is recognised as the chemist who first isolated carbon dioxide.

Born in Uddingston, Lanarkshire, in 1924, Sir James Whyte Black has contributed to the world of medicine through his development of a range of important drugs, including one to treat coronary heart disease. He was awarded the Nobel Prize for Medicine in 1988.

Although the names Blackadder, Blackburn, Blackmore, and Blackwell only relate to one another in that they all contain the suffix 'Black', they may be considered part of a 'Black' kindred, and it is appropriate to note the achievements of those who have borne the proud names down through the centuries.

Contrary to popular opinion, 'Blackadder' does not refer to a dark coloured and venomous snake, but derives from the Old English 'awedur', meaning a stream, or running water.

There is a Blackadder Water and a small village of Blackadder in the Scottish Borders, and a family of that name held lands there for centuries.

These lands were lost, some say through treachery, to the Homes of Wedderburn following the battle of Flodden in 1513.

Notable Blackadders include the Rev. John Blackadder (1615-1686), the Covenanting minister who preached at banned open-air conventicles in Dumfriesshire before he was outlawed in 1674.

He spent some time in exile in Holland before returning to Scotland and later dying in imprisonment on the Bass Rock.

In contemporary times, Elizabeth Violet Blackadder, born in 1931, is the celebrated Scottish painter and printmaker who is also the first woman to have been elected to the prestigious Royal Scottish Academy and the Royal Academy.

In the world of sport, Todd Blackadder, born in 1971, was a popular New Zealand rugby player in the 1990s, and at one time a captain of the All Blacks.

'Blackburn' is a location name, indicating the site of a dark stream, or burn, and Blackburn, in Lancashire, is the most noted place of the name, while a number of Blackburns have achieved distinction.

They include Arthur Seaforth Blackburn (1892-1960), who was born at Woodville, South Australia, and was awarded the Victoria Cross for his bravery in action during the First World War, and fellow Australian Doris Blackburn (1889-1970), who was an activist for women's rights and peace issues and a member of the Australian Parliament.

Jonathan Blackburn (1700-1765) was a gifted American portrait painter, while Tony Blackburn, born in Surrey in 1943, is a popular British disc jockey and entertainer.

'Blackmore' is Moorish in origin, stemming from 'blackamoor', meaning someone of dark, or swarthy, appearance, and famous Blackmores include Richard Doddridge Blackmore (1825-1900), better known as *Lorna Doone* author R.D. Blackmore.

Sir Richard Blackmore (1654-1729) was a distinguished English physician and poet, while Ritchie Blackmore, born in 1945, is the acclaimed British rock guitarist noted for his work with bands such as Deep Purple and Rainbow.

'Blackwell' is another location name, derived from the site of a well that was described as black either because of the inky depths of its waters or because it was situated in a dark and lonely spot.

Many of these wells were sites of ancient pagan worship until they became venerated in later times as sacred Christian sites.

The daughter of a wealthy London family, Elizabeth Blackwell (1821-1910) immigrated to America and became the first woman to practice medicine in that nation.

Active in the anti-slavery movement, along with her brother, Henry, she was also the founder, in 1857, of the New York Infirmary for Indigent Women and Children, trained nurses during the American Civil War, and founded the Women's Medical College.

She returned to England in 1869 and, along with Florence Nightingale, opened the Women's Medical College. She was also the first female physician to be recorded in the UK Medical Register.

In contemporary times, Chris Blackwell, born in 1937, is the businessman and founder of Island Records, the label that signed the late Jamaican reggae star Bob Marley.